Contents

IT HAD A FROG IN ITS THROAT.

ISBN 978-0-545-80649-7

12 11 10 9 8 7 6 5 4 3 2 1   15 16 17 18 19 20/0

Printed in the U.S.A.   132
First edition, January 2015

S-s-scary?

Are snakes cool? Or creepy? Here's the good news: Most snakes won't hurt you. The rest? Be afraid. Some snakes kill with a single bite. Others *squeeeeze* their victims to death. In this book, you'll see some of the coolest snakes around—and you'll be totally safe!

ICKY STICKY STICKERS

Have you read that? Now stick this! A tiger snake can kill you with one bite.

SCHOLASTIC

icky sticky readers

Scary Snakes

Laaren Brown

SCHOLASTIC INC.

New York   Toronto   London   Auckland
Sydney   Mexico City   New Delhi   Hong Kong

Dear family *and friends* ∧ of new readers,

Welcome to Icky Sticky Readers, part of the Scholastic Reader program. At Scholastic, we have taken over ninety years' worth of experience with teachers, parents, and children and put it into a program that is designed to match your child's interest and skills. Scholastic Readers are designed to support your child's efforts to learn how to read at every age and every stage.

LEVEL 1 READER
- Beginning Reader
- Preschool–Grade 1
- Sight words
- Words to sound out
- Simple sentences

LEVEL 2 READER
- Developing Reader
- Grades 1–2
- New vocabulary
- Longer sentences

LEVEL 3 READER
- Growing Reader
- Grades 1–3
- Reading for inspiration and information

For ideas about sharing books with your new reader, please visit www.scholastic.com. Enjoy helping your child learn to read and love to read!

Happy reading!

Francie Alexander
Chief Academic Officer
Scholastic Inc.

WHY COULDN'T THE SNAKE TALK?

ICKY STICKY STICKERS

Every time you see this sign, look for a sticker to fill the space!

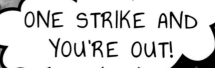

ONE STRIKE AND YOU'RE OUT!

This is a parrot snake. It eats birds!

Here's another thing that makes snakes scary: They love to hide. There are nearly 3,000 types of snake, and they turn up all over the place. In the ground. In the water. Even gliding through the air! *Aaaaaaggghhh!*

in the ground

in the water

in the air

WE'RE EVERYWHERE.

HERE.

Strange places to find a snake: boots and shoes, cars and planes, trash cans and closets, bathtubs and toilets. Strange—but TRUE.

WELCOME TO YOUR WORST NIGHTMARE!

ICKY STICKY STICKERS

Have you read that? Now stick this! Rattlesnakes like to hang out in the desert!

EVEN HERE.

HERE.

Deadly bodies

Snakes are perfect killing machines.

They are bendy.
Really bendy.
That's because
they have LOTS of
bones. This deadly tube
can twist itself around a
branch—or its prey's body.

ICKY STICKY STICKERS

Have you read that? Now stick this! A corn snake can tie itself into a knot.

THAT'S KNOT FUNNY!

prey
pray
An animal that is hunted and eaten by another animal.

New word

200 to 400: ➡
the number of bones in a snake's back

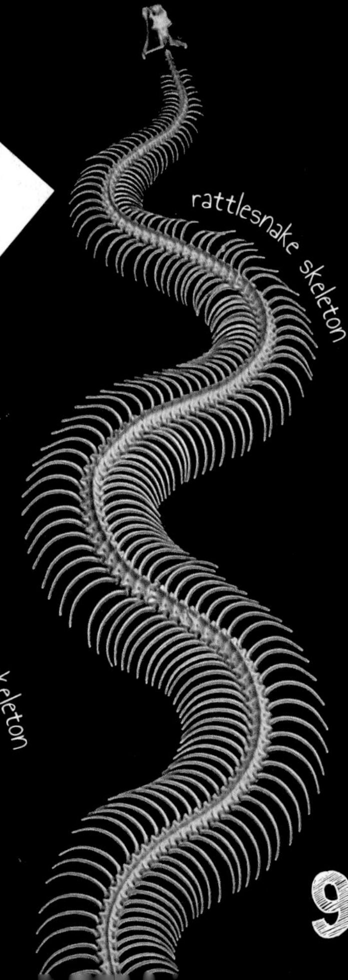

rattlesnake skeleton

33: ➡
the number of bones in your back

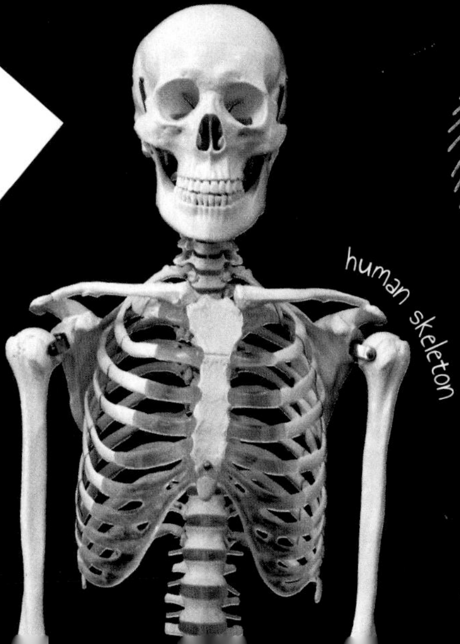

human skeleton

9

How long is your school bus? Long, right? Now imagine a snake that long! Good news: The very longest snakes lived millions of years ago. Bad news: There are still a lot of huge snakes out there. Maybe not quite as long as a bus—but long enough to scare you!

10 How LONG?

blue whale: 98 feet

The longest!

reticulated python:
26 feet

green anaconda:
22 feet

Burmese python:
18 feet

ICKY STICKY STICKERS

Have you read that? Now stick this! Is this anaconda yawning? I sure hope so!

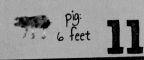

saltwater crocodile:
23 feet

African elephant:
16 feet

human:
6 feet

pig:
6 feet

Snakes are tough. Like armor, their skin is made up of lots of small, hard scales. A snake's skin doesn't grow with the rest of its body. So, a few times a year, the snake sheds its old skin and grows a new, bigger one.

  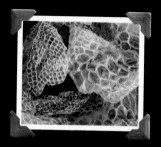

 Time to shed! The snake's eyes get cloudy.

 The snake rubs against a rock. Its old skin splits.

 It wriggles free, leaving its old skin behind.

UM . . . HAVE YOU SEEN MY TAIL?

What's the fastest thing on no feet? A snake! Some snakes can reach speeds of 12 miles per hour! But most don't move that fast unless they are in danger. Snakes use their rough belly scales to grip surfaces, and their muscles to

CREEPING

SIDEWINDING

ICKY STICKY STICKERS

Have you read that? Now stick this! The black mamba is the world's fastest snake.

push themselves along. Some snakes creep forward in a straight line. Other snakes move in an S shape, winding from side to side or slithering.

WHY IS A SNAKE HARD TO FOOL?

YOU CAN'T PULL ITS LEG!

SLITHERING

15

How snakes kill

Snakes can smell
really well—with their tongues!
A snake uses its forked tongue
to pick up scents from the air.
Those scents tell the snake when
dinner is near.

Have you read that? Now stick this! A king cobra can sense prey over 330 feet away.

Like heat-seeking missiles, some snakes can sense the warmth of prey's bodies.

Shhhh! Was that a rattle? It could be a rattlesnake, warning you to STAY AWAY. You should. More than 300 kinds of snake are full of a type of poison called venom . . . and the rattlesnake is one of them! When it bites, venom flows down its fangs and into its prey. Some

THESE
SNAKES
ARE
FULL
OF
VENOM:

DEATH ADDER

COBRA

TIGER SNAKE

venom stops your heart from beating. Some venom makes your blood clot. Some venom stops your breathing. Venom is nature's best killer. So STAY AWAY from that rattlesnake!

S-s-s-say it!

venom
VEN-uhm
Poison made by some snakes, used to kill prey.

New word

ICKY STICKY STICKERS
Have you read that? Now stick this! A Gaboon viper has longer fangs than any other snake.

SEA SNAKE   MAMBA   VIPER   TAIPAN

Other snakes just love to hug. In fact, a snake may hug its prey SO hard, it squeezes it to death! Snakes that hug are called constrictors. A constrictor grabs its prey with its teeth and wrap its coils around its victim. It squeezes tighter and tighter and tighter. . . . Soon the prey can't breathe. Way too much hugging!

AM I INTERRUPTING? EX-SQUEEZE ME!

ICKY STICKY STICKERS

Have you read that? Now stick this! A boa constrictor can sense its prey's heartbeat.

Open your mouth. Wide. Wider . . . just a little bit wider . . . Forget it. Snakes win. Snakes' jaws are not fixed together at the back, so they can take in snacks that are bigger than their heads. Snakes don't eat very often, but when they do—look out!

ICKY STICKY STICKERS

Have you read that? Now stick this! An African rock python can eat an antelope. WHOLE.

They can swallow very **BIG** prey. Eggs? *Mmmm.* Rats? Yum! Bunnies? Yes, please! Goats? You better *baaaaa*–lieve it.

COME ON, TURN THE PAGE. I'M WAITING FOR YOU.

Guess what this snake had for lunch!

23

Born scary

Most snakes are
REALLY BAD parents.
Some mother snakes lay soft-
shelled eggs, then slither away. Some give
birth to live young, then slither away. Good
thing baby snakes are born tough. They soon
learn to eat small, weak animals and hide
from big, strong animals. If they get
this wrong, THEY DIE!

**ICKY
STICKY
STICKERS**

Have you read that?
Now stick this!
A baby
copperhead's
bite might not kill
you. Or it might!

hatchling
HACH-ling
A baby that
came out
of an egg.

New word

snakes born from eggs

snakes born alive

Here's a handful
of trouble!

TOP 10 deadly snakes

We've saved the scariest for last. Here are the ten deadliest snakes. Nothing is safe from them! They strike faster than lightning. They're packed with superstrong venom. If you see one of them, BACK OFF!

I'M A KILLER!

GLUB GLUB!

2 Dubois' sea snake

1 inland taipan

Medal winners

ICKY STICKY STICKERS

Have you read that? Now stick this! Saw-scaled vipers kill thousands of people each year.

SHOW-OFF.

3 eastern brown snake

Runners-up

4 black mamba

5 black tiger snake

6 king cobra

7 saw-scaled viper

8 fer-de-lance

9 common death adder

10 eastern diamondback rattlesnake

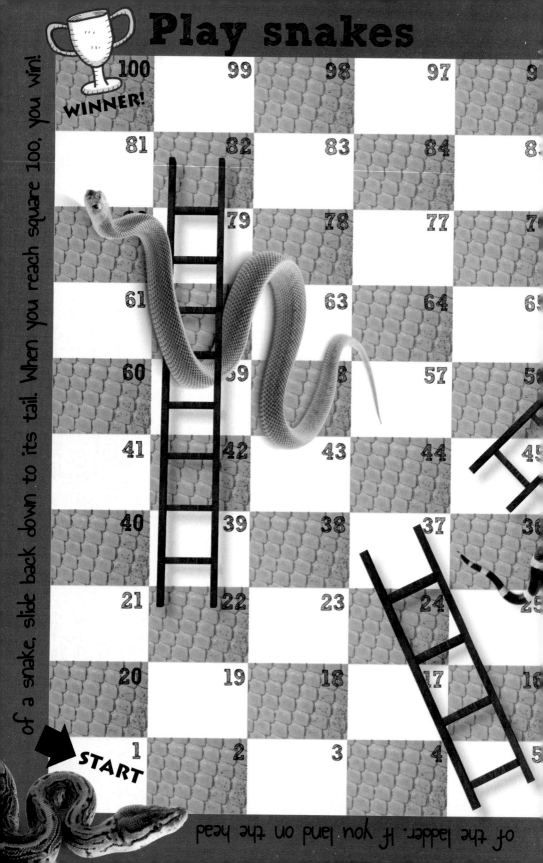

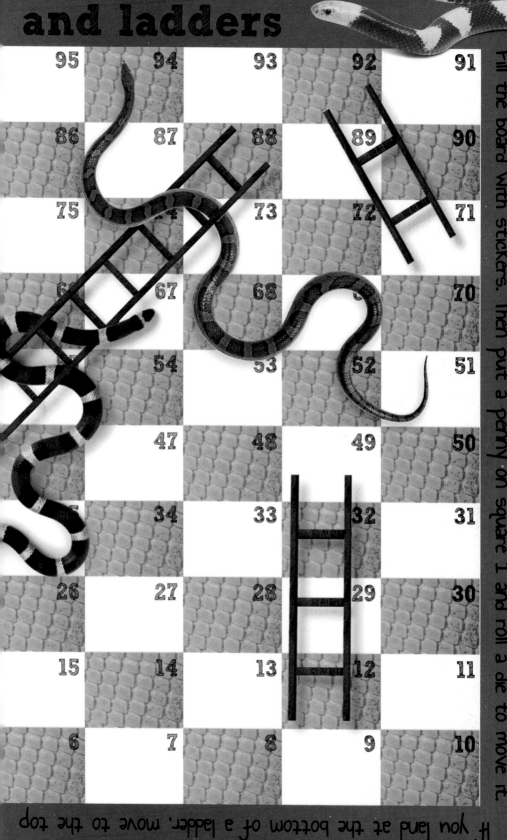

Glossary

clot
For a liquid, like blood, to become thicker. Clots in your blood can be dangerous.

coil
A loop or series of loops, like those made by a snake's body.

constrictor
A type of snake that squeezes its prey to death.

creep
To move very slowly and carefully, so as not to make noise. Some snakes can creep forward in a straight line.

desert
An area where there is very little rain and hardly any plants grow.

fang
An animal's long, pointed tooth.

forked tongue
A tongue that splits into two parts at the tip.

hatchling
A baby that came out of an egg.

jaw
One of the two bones that surround the mouth and hold the teeth in place.

muscle
Body tissue that pulls on bones to make them move.

prey
An animal that is hunted and eaten by another animal.

scale
A thin, flat piece of hard skin on an animal's body.

scent
A smell, like that of a hunted animal.

shed
To get rid of old outer skin so that the animal inside can grow bigger.

sidewind

To move diagonally forward in a series of flat, S-shaped curves. Some snakes sidewind when they move across desert sands.

skeleton

The set of bones that supports and protects the bodies of some animals.

skin

The thin outer covering on the body of a person or animal.

slither

To move along by sliding, like a snake.

swallow

To make food or drink move from the mouth to the stomach.

venom

Poison made by some animals, used to kill prey. Snakes pass venom to their prey by biting them.

S-S-SO, NOW YOU KNOW ALL ABOUT S-S-SNAKES.

THE END!

31

Index

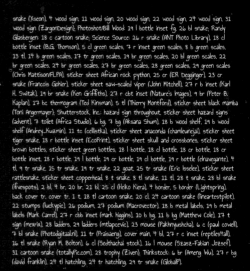

Image credits

Alamy Images: 5 tr (Aamod Zambre/ephotocorp), 1 main, 12, 13 bg (Daniel Heuclin/ Nature Picture Library), 16 main snake head, 17 main snake head (David Chapman), 5 cr (Robert Pickett/Papilio), 7 t snake (Stephen Dalton/Nature Picture Library), Bryn Walls: 9 tr magnifying glass, 15 tr magnifying glass, 19 tr magnifying glass, 25 tr magnifying glass; Dreamstime: back cover cl (Amwu), back cover cr (Isselee), 19 cl bottle inset (Mgkuijpers); Fotolia: 29 c snake (bramgino), 29 l snake (Eric Isselee); Getty Images: 25 b, 32 (Justin Sanson/Newspix), 27 bl snake (Kristian Bell), 5 bl (Martin Harvey), 6 cr (Tim Laman); iStockphoto: sticker sheet cl gray snake, 16 r crickets (2happy), 14 bl cactus (3drenderings), 3 gold frame (4x6), 16 r larvae (akova), 2 bg, 3 bg, 14 bg, 17 bg, 30 b, 31 b bg (alxpin), sticker sheet boa constrictor (amattel), sticker sheet tc green snake, sticker sheet tc striped snake, sticker sheet tl brown snake, sticker sheet cl colorful snake, sticker sheet cr coiled snake, sticker sheet bl white snake, sticker sheet bc black snake, 7 br snake, 14 br snake, 15 b snake (amwu), 15 br cactus, 16 tl ant, 16 tl ant, 22 frog (Antagain), 20 tl (Baksiabat), 22 moss, 23 moss (Barcin), 24 tall grass, 25 tall grass (bgfoto), 17 br gerbil (CamiloTorres), 8 b sign, 14 b sign (chapin31), 11 b elephant (Clawdad), 6 bct (colematt), 11 b human (DRB Images, LLC), 9 bl (dreamnikon), 5 br (eROMAZe), 16 r lizard (garymilner), sticker sheet tr brown coiled snake (gehutka), sticker sheet tl snake, sticker sheet tr striped snake, sticker sheet corn snake, sticker sheet king cobra, sticker sheet br green snake, sticker sheet br yellow snake, sticker sheet bc yellow snake, sticker sheet bc coiled snake, 11 b piglet, 16 l fish, 24 t bg, 25 t bg (GlobalP), photo corners throughout (hanbaram), 16 tl ant (Henrik_L), 22 lizard (icuIizard), 19 l bottle inset bg (ifish), 26 bl bowl (Irochka_T), 3 t snake, 30 t, 31 t (isarescheewin), 23 tr snake (johnaudrey), 16 bl eggs (JohnnyMad), 7 toilet paper (Kone), 16 tr frog (Lezh), sticker sheet cl brown snake (litnik), 20 bg, 21 bg (macroris), 14 t snake (mario31), 14 t cl bg, 15 c bg (michaklootwijk), 13 tr (Mikosch), 6 bl (mmpile), 10 b whale (MR1805), 18 cobra (omega977), sticker sheet tl gray snake (Ornitolog82), 27 r cbt inset (ParentesiGrafica), 14 r inset sand, 14 tl sand, 15 br sand (photka), 24 b bg, 25 b bg (redmal), 3 b snake (reptiles4all), white frame throughout (Rouzes), 14 b crocodile (seaskylab), 14 b bg, 15 b bg (skodonnell), 27 r ctb inset (skynavin), sticker sheet Gaboon viper, 5 bc, 13 tc, 27 r t inset (Snowleopard1), 16 white plate (sorendls), sticker sheet tc gray snake (texcroc), 22 rabbit, 23 rabbit (tilo), 10 t bg, 11 t bg (timsa), 6 bcb (Vasiliki Varvaki), 23 bird nest (WoodenDinosaur), 21 tr

snake (Xseon), 4 wood sign, 11 wood sign, 20 wood sign, 22 wood sign, 24 wood sign, 31 wood sign (ZargonDesign); Photoshot/Bill Wood: 19 l bottle inset fg, 26 bl snake; Randy Glasbergen: 18 c cartoon snake; Science Source: 26 r snake (ANT Photo Library), 18 cl bottle inset (B.G. Thomson), 5 cl green scales, 7 r inset green scales, 8 b green scales, 13 tl, 14 b green scales, 17 tr green scales, 19 br green scales, 20 bl green scales, 22 br green scales, 24 br green scales, 27 br green scales, 28 green scales, 29 green scales (Chris Mattison/FLPA), sticker sheet African rock python, 25 cr (ER Degginger), 23 cr snake (Francois Gohier), sticker sheet saw-scaled viper (John Mitchell), 27 r b inset (Karl H. Switak), 19 br snake (Ken Griffiths), 27 r cbt inset (Nature's Images), 9 br (Peter B. Kaplan), 17 bc thermogram (Ted Kinsman), 5 tl (Thierry Montford), sticker sheet black mamba (Toni Angermayer); Shutterstock, Inc.: hazard sign throughout, sticker sheet hazard signs (advent), 7 toilet (Africa Studio), 6 bg, 7 bg (Aksana Shum), 18 b wood shelf, 19 b wood shelf (Andrey_Kuzmin), 11 tc (cellistka), sticker sheet anaconda (chamkeunejai), sticker sheet tiger snake, 18 r bottle inset (EcoPrint), sticker sheet skull and crossbones, sticker sheet brown bottles, sticker sheet green bottles, 18 l bottle, 18 cl bottle, 19 cr bottle, 18 cr bottle inset, 18 r bottle, 19 l bottle, 19 cr bottle, 19 cl bottle, 19 r bottle (chavegante), 4 tl, 9 tr snake, 15 tr snake, 19 tr snake, 22 goat, 25 tr snake (Eric Isselee), sticker sheet rattlesnake, sticker sheet copperhead, 8 t snake, 9 tl snake, 11 tl, 28 t snake, 28 bl snake (fivespots), 2 bl, 4 br, 20 br, 21 bl, 25 cl (Heiko Kiera), 4 border, 5 border (Lightspring), back cover tr, cover tr, 1 t, 18 tl cartoon snake, 20 cl, 24 cartoon snake (lineartestpilot), 22 stumps (luckypic), 26 podium, 27 podium (Macrovector), 18 b metal labels, 19 b metal labels (Mark Carrel), 27 r cbb inset (mark higgins), 10 b bg, 11 b bg (Matthew Cole), 17 t sign (mexrix), 28 ladders, 29 ladders (mtlapcevic), 23 mouse (Pakhnyushcha), 6 c (paul cowell), 7 bl snake (Photodigitaal.nl), 11 tr (Praisaeng), cover main, 4 bl, 27 r c inset (reptiles4all), 16 tl snake (Ryan M. Bolton), 6 cl (Sedthachai stock), 16 l mouse (Szasz-Fabian Jozsef), 31 cartoon snake (totallyPic.com), 28 trophy (Ziven); Thinkstock: 6 br (Ameng Wu), 27 r bg (david franklin), 24 tl hatchling, 24 bl hatchling, 29 tr snake (GlobalP).

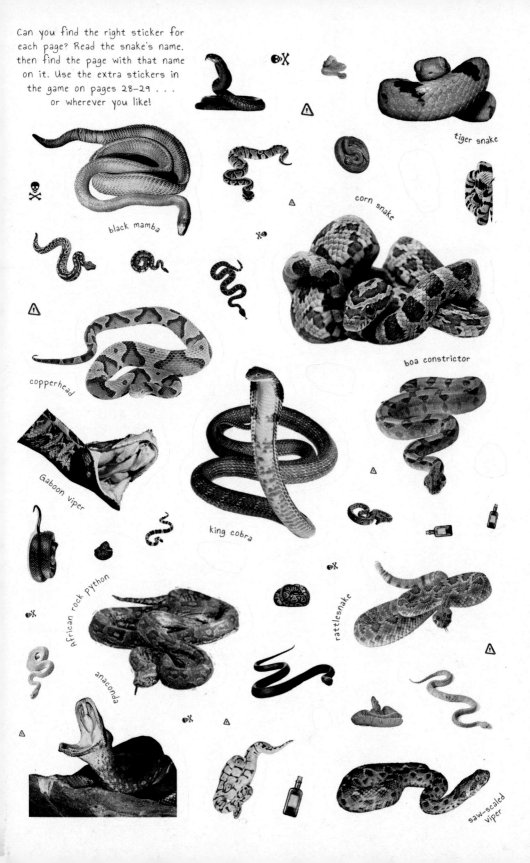

Can you find the right sticker for each page? Read the snake's name, then find the page with that name on it. Use the extra stickers in the game on pages 28–29 . . . or wherever you like!

tiger snake

black mamba

corn snake

copperhead

boa constrictor

Gaboon viper

king cobra

African rock python

rattlesnake

anaconda

saw-scaled viper